BOURKE'S
PARAKEETS

DOREEN HAGGARD

CONTENTS

ACKNOWLEDGEMENTS

With special thanks to all the people who helped me put this book together, especially:

• Andy Haggard, my husband, for being my photographer and for all the help and encouragement he has given me during this adventure;
• Fred Jackett and Colin Jeal, photographers;
• Ian Marshall, who has supplied some very helpful information;
• Joan Kaley, for allowing me to photograph her yellow Bourke's parakeets;
• Jonathan Coote, for letting me photograph his aviaries.

I had the idea of writing this book when I first started keeping Bourke's parakeets and realised what brilliant birds they are. I hope you will enjoy reading it as much as I have enjoyed writing it.

Introduction

The Bourke's grass parakeet can be found in the wild in the Australian continent, in an area stretching right across from Western Australia in the west to southwestern Queensland and the western parts of New South Wales in the east. They are also found on the island of Tasmania. They were observed in various locations within their range from 1845 to 1910, and then no more sightings were reported until 1936 and 1938, when a flock of about 100 birds was observed in Southern Australia. It has been noted that a flock of Bourke's parakeets may remain in one area for some years before migrating, as a unit, to another locality.

In 1853 the Bourke's parakeet was discovered in New South Wales by Sir Thomas Mitchell, and the species was named after Dr Richard Bourke, the state governor. Its Latin name according to the binomial system is *Neopsephotus bourkii*, but other common names for it are the pink-bellied parakeet, the blue-vented parakeet, the night parrot and the sundown parrot. Several colour mutations are bred today in captivity, the

The Bourke has a lovely, quiet nature and is very trusting

most favoured being the rosa Bourke with its rich, deep rose colouring, but the normal and the yellow are also beautiful birds.

John Gould was the first person to draw the Bourke and describe its nature and habits in detail. The species reportedly reached London for the first time in 1876, and the birds were imported into Germany in large numbers in the same year: they are known to the Germans as *Bourkesittich* (normal) and *Rosenbauchsittich* (rosa).

In 1958 the Bourke's parakeet nearly became extinct in the wild. Some ornithologists felt that there was a connection with intensive sheep farming in the areas that they inhabited, since millions of sheep were kept on the grasslands, depleting the natural food supplies of the Bourke's parakeets. Then, after a long drought that killed off large numbers of sheep, the Bourke population increased again. Numbers have only fully recovered in recent years, but there is certainly no fear of extinction now.

Bourke's parakeets fly close to the ground, and will only travel short distances, except when in search of food. They nest in trees, in holes one to three metres above the ground. They lay their eggs on rotten wood collected in the bottom of these holes, not gathering their own nesting materials. The hen lays four to five eggs in one clutch and, during the incubation period, she is fed by the cock. Their preferred habitats are mulga woodlands, but they also live in open bushland where they can find their food: for example, seeds of shrubs, grasses, herbaceous plants, and acacia and cassia seeds.

Bourkes search for food in the early morning and late afternoon, keeping in the shade in the hours of hot sunshine between 10.00 am and 4.00 pm. There are no reports of Bourkes cross-breeding with other species of parakeet, and there are no closely related species. It is to be hoped that their numbers do not decline again as their home areas become more heavily populated by humans.

The Bourke has a lovely, quiet nature and is very trusting. It has been increasingly favoured as a household pet in recent years, and is becoming very popular with breeders and fanciers because, among many other good points, it has a pleasant, mellow voice, breeds easily and is easily tamed.

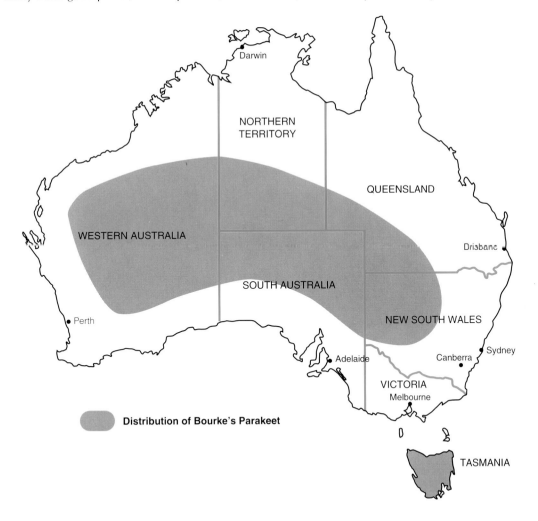

Map showing the distribution of Bourke's parakeets in the wild

GETTING TO KNOW YOUR BOURKE'S PARAKEET

Three colour varieties of Bourke: yellow (left), normal (centre) and rosa (right)

COLOUR VARIETIES OF BOURKE'S PARAKEETS

As has already been said, three colour varieties of the Bourke's parakeet are commonly kept in captivity today: the normal and the two most common mutations, rosa and yellow.

Normal

The normal Bourke's parakeet is a very colourful bird, the most noticeable colour being sky blue. It has dark grey down the centre of its back extending to the edge of its wings, where the dark grey is replaced by stunning sky blue edging. The lower part of the breast is bright salmon pink, fading to grey with hints of blue. The inside tail feathers are green, with light blue blended with grey-brown on the outside feathers. The primary wing feathers are a beautiful, deep, violet blue. The eyes are dark brown. The cock has brownish upper parts, pinkish red under parts and blue flanks, brow and eyebrow stripes, and patches under the eyes. He also has a small amount of blue on top of his head that blends in with a light grey-brown mask, and his nostrils are black. The female is generally paler in colour, and without the blue brow band. She has a dark grey mask and her nostrils are brown in colour. The shape of the heads is different, the hen's being much flatter than the cock's, providing a good method of sexing them before their adult plumage is complete.

Rosa

In my opinion, this is the most beautiful of the Bourke family. It is certainly the most eye-catching, with its deep, rich, rose colouring and its grey mask. It is a sex-linked colour mutation, which has made it easy to fix without adversely affecting the bird's size and stamina.

The rosa Bourke is predominantly a rich rose pink in colour. At the end of its wings a beautiful shade of blue blends with white edging, outlined in dark grey feathers with lighter grey shading to the ends of some of the feathers. Its eyes are dark brown. The hen's mask is darker grey than the cock's and more diamond-shaped, and this is the easiest way of sexing them. She also has more scaly markings.

Yellow
The yellow is a beautiful soft yellow buff on the back of the wings and upper tail feathers, with the head, neck and breast a soft rosy pink, lower underparts dull yellow and a little yellow around its eyes. The eyes are dark red or dark brown. The hen's colours are much duller than those of the cock, but otherwise similar.

Other mutations
Although these are the colours most commonly found in captivity, there are other mutations. These include the Isobel (more rosy pink extending down the back) and the cinnamon (similar to the normal, but with reddish eyes).

BOURKE VITAL STATISTICS
As can be seen from the descriptions, the female Bourke's parakeet is generally much duller than the male, showing less blue. She is also usually smaller.

A rosa Bourke: in my opinion, the most beautiful variety

A yellow Bourke

The Bourke's parakeet has a remarkable average body length of 19cm. The adult male Bourke's parakeet's wing span is 106–120mm (average: 114mm) to the female's 108–119mm (average: 112mm), and he has a tail length of 98–110mm (average: 105mm). The cock's body weight is 47–49g to the hen's 42–49g.

BOURKES AS PETS

Perhaps you have decided that you want to keep just one Bourke's parakeet, or a pair of them, as special pets in a cage in your house. In this case, you will need to tame them to appreciate them fully. Bourkes are quite easy to tame and I have noticed that' the rosa Bourke is the easiest. The hen squawks a little when you approach her and she might give a little nip, although it will not hurt too much. The cock is completely different: he has a lovely temperament and handles very well. He does not seem to have any fear of humans and is not at all aggressive.

The wing span of a Bourke

When you first bring your young Bourke into the home it is always best to let it settle in for a day or so. It may be suffering from stress; this is very common in birds that have changed their environment. Taming a bird takes a great deal of time and patience. Your voice is the tool for training the bird, and your bird must get used to it before it can accept you as a friend. You will not get anywhere if you frighten it. At this stage, only one person should undertake the taming. Otherwise, your bird will become confused and you will achieve nothing. Talk to the Bourke through the cage bars in a soft voice. This will calm it a little and it will soon learn to recognise your voice. With the cage door slightly open you can offer it some treats. Move very slowly, talking softly, and do not make any sudden movements.

When you are trying to tame a bird, one problem often encountered is that it keeps flying off your finger onto the floor. This can become frustrating but, if you clip the bird's wings (see Chapter 4), it will eventually settle down and become easier to work with when it realises it cannot fly any more. Its wings will grow back after the next moult.

Bourkes enjoy a spray of millet or a small piece of apple as a treat. They will soon accept treats from your hand and each time they will become more aware that you are not going to harm them. I have found Bourkes the easiest of all parakeets to train. They are very inquisitive and alert birds and you will not go wrong by having one as a family pet. With some species, it is impossible to tame a bird that has been left in the aviary for more than a year as it is too accustomed to its comparative freedom. However, this is certainly not true in the case of the rosa Bourke's parakeet. The first taming session should not take longer than 10–15 minutes; otherwise the bird will lose interest. Complete quiet is required with no intrusions or disturbances. A tamed bird that has lost fear of humans becomes hardier than the aviary birds and therefore more resilient to illnesses.

It is always best to keep your Bourkes in pairs as they like the comfort of a partner. You must be careful where you position their cage as they do not like draughty locations. They prefer not to be kept in a room by themselves, enjoying company.

Bourke's parakeets are very calm by nature and pleasant birds to have as pets. In fact, given the Bourke's overwhelming qualities, you could not ask for more in a pet. If you are convinced, and decide to keep them, I hope you enjoy them as much as I do.

BOURKES AS AVIARY BIRDS

Bourkes breed better when kept in an aviary on their own as they like their privacy at such times. Most species become more aggressive during the breeding season. If you have to use a mixed aviary you can put in a few finches or maybe cockatiels as these are known to get on with each other. Do not mix them with lovebirds, as these have a habit of destroying any nest other than their own. I have also heard reports that budgerigars are not a good suggestion for a mixed aviary as they too have been known to interfere with other species.

A small aviary about 2m x 1m (6ft x 3ft) is appropriate for one pair. Whilst breeding, it is not advisable to keep more than one pair of Bourkes together, as the cock bird can become very protective of his mate and too busy defending her honour to breed. I have kept cockatiels and finches in the same aviary as Bourkes for years, and they seem to leave each other alone. However, if you are keeping your Bourkes with cockatiels, make sure the Bourkes' nest box entrance is too small for the cockatiels, or they may try to nest in the wrong box.

In a mixed aviary Bourkes keep themselves to themselves, not annoying any other species. Bourkes do not require much room in the aviary; they need more length than width so that they can span their wings and have the length for flight. Watching them in flight is quite amazing. They will dive down towards the floor, and then up towards the perches, making a twittering sound as they fly. They seldom fly in a straight line across the aviary. They often sit close together on the perches just enjoying each other's company.

Given the Bourke's overwhelming qualities, I don't think you could ask for more in a pet bird

SELECTION AND PURCHASE

Bourkes are becoming more popular today than they were previously, but there are still many people who do not recognise one when they see it. They tend to think that it is a budgerigar.

When buying your Bourke from your local pet shop or aviary centre, you must be aware of some vital signs of illnesses. Always ask the shop assistant to catch the bird for you and hold it in front of you so that you can examine it for the following:

Eyes: If a Bourke is unhealthy its eyes will be dull and oval in shape. Healthy eyes are clear and round.

Vent: Another sign of a sick bird is a dirty vent (anus).

Feathers: A bird that never seems to preen itself is an unhealthy bird.

Fluffed up: If it is all fluffed up and sitting on the bottom of the cage it may be in stress.

You must be aware of what signs to look for before purchasing your bird. Most pet shops will give you 48 hours to return a sick

A good way of keeping Bourkes: an aviary with small flights (2m x 1m)

bird. However, I would strongly recommend buying a bird from someone you know if possible, so that you can be fairly sure you will get a healthy one. You normally cannot determine the correct age of a Bourke, and you may need this information, but pet shop staff will not necessarily be able to tell you.

If you are buying a breeding pair of Bourke's parakeets make sure they are unrelated. It might be better to buy from two different dealers. If your Bourkes are related you may have problems resulting from interbreeding. Even if the eggs are fertile, the chicks are often found dead in the shell. They may never become fully feathered and they are quite likely to be improperly formed, so probably they will die naturally.

Age

There is no way of telling the age of a Bourke's parakeet simply by looking at it: I have never seen an old-looking Bourke! The best way to be sure is to obtain it from someone you know. Your local pet shop has probably bought its stock in bulk from breeders, so will have no idea of the age of individual birds. However, if the bird has been closed-ringed its ring will be clearly marked with its year of birth and its breeder's initials and, since Bourkes cannot be closed-ringed much after six days old, you will know its age from this. The lifespan of a Bourke's parakeet in captivity is eight to twelve years, though some have been known to live a little longer.

EQUIPMENT

Before leaving the shop where you bought your Bourke, make sure you have the necessary requirements for your bird, such as cuttlebone, mineral block, grit and small parakeet mix. Worm your Bourke and spray it for mites as soon as you get it home. Do not put your new Bourke straight into the aviary but keep it apart for the first day to make sure it is healthy, not suffering from stress or disease.

AVIARIES

Bourke's parakeets are strong fliers and do quite well in small aviaries or flights. As has already been said, the smallest size for a breeding pair would be 1m x 2m (3ft x 6ft). A larger one of 3m x 1.3m (10ft x 4ft) would be perfectly adequate for two pairs. Long aviaries allow for flight and all birds need flight and exercise for good breeding condition. However, it is best not to keep two pairs of Bourkes in the same aviary when they are breeding. When they are not breeding (the winter months are out of season for the Bourke) you can have many pairs in one aviary without any problems at all. On the whole, they are peaceful neighbours.

You will need to decide on the floor covering for your aviary. Three possibilities are woodchip, stones or plain concrete base. My aviaries are indoor ones in sheds and I prefer to use woodchip on the floor. I change the floor materials every week and clean out with disinfectant. You must also clean your water and seed dishes at least once a week to keep down the risk of infection. Fresh water should be constantly available, to which you can add vitamins every few months to assure good health. I also have large water containers for the birds to bathe in, which can be shallow clay pots. Not many Bourkes like to bathe but, if you are keeping other birds in the aviary, a small bathing water dish is advisable. Perches should be taken down regularly and scrubbed, or even replaced. By keeping a clean aviary you minimise risk of infection and disease, which are often fostered by neglect. This can result in heartbreak: the loss of all your birds.

Outdoor aviaries should have part of the roof covered with a sturdy waterproof covering to provide shade in summer and shelter in winter. A concrete floor is advisable as this is easy to wash down and will keep out rodents.

An aviary centre displaying birds in a mixed aviary

Natural perches from trees are good for your birds, but make sure they are clean and free from pesticides

Have an enclosed section attached to your aviary into which you can drive the birds during bad weather. Bourkes do not like the wind and rain. The sheltered, enclosed section is ideal for your nest boxes.

Another good idea for your aviary is a porch fixed to the outside door, allowing you to enter the porch and shut the outside door before entering the main door of the aviary. This helps to prevent your birds from escaping. I have seen many birds escape from the aviary when there is no safety door, which is easy to fit and very efficient. Having the second door could save you many birds over the months.

You must take care when storing your seed in outside sheds and aviaries. Clean dustbins are suitable for a large amount of seed. Keep all your seed dry and do not give your birds seed that is damp or wet as it could be mouldy. Make sure it is all in sealed containers to keep out mice. Be warned: if you do have rodents in the vicinity, they will find a way in. Try to keep seed off the floor so that the mice cannot get to it. I would suggest seed hoppers as these are mounted, so keep the seed off the floor and out of the reach of rodents.

If you have a problem with rodents you will have to take drastic measures to keep them out of the aviary. Rats or mice urinating on the aviary floor can spread disease. This is potentially lethal for Bourkes, who are floor feeders. Rodents have also been known to get into nest boxes and frighten the birds. Clean the aviary at least once a week and check it regularly. As a last resort you can use rat poison, but do make sure you do not put it where your birds or any other pets can eat it. Remove your birds from the aviary to do this properly and clean it out before returning them. Rat poison is expensive but very efficient.

Some breeders have wooden shelves or ledges on which to put their seed trays. Make sure they are not in line with the perches, in case the birds foul the seed trays.

Bourkes like apple tree branches for perches but make sure these have not been sprayed with chemicals such as insecticides. It is very important to keep your perches clean as Bourkes are prone to eye infections and, if not treated, these will spread rapidly (see Chapter 5).

With indoor aviaries you can fit lights, which is a good idea for early spring breeding, as you can put the light on about 6.00 am until it is light and then again at 5.00 pm until 9.00 pm. Use a dimmer switch, as natural light decreases gradually, and be careful about turning the light off completely in case the hen is out of her nest box and cannot find her way back to her eggs or chicks.

Heaters can be fitted during the colder weather. There are several types on the market today, including a heater and light combined, but this is very expensive.

If you have an indoor aviary that has been converted from a shed, remember that birds need light. Plenty of windows must be cut in and covered with netting, but do make sure you block them during the winter to exclude the draughts. If you use plastic for this you will not shut out too much light. I have glass windows fitted during the winter with mesh covering them. Then in the summer I can take out the glass to give my birds plenty of fresh air.

The door too can be adjusted to the weather. I have an aviary panel door on the inside and a shed door on the outside. In the summer I leave the shed door open to circulate the air, while the aviary panel keeps cats out; cats can be rather too interested in aviaries. A fan with some sort of guard around it placed nearby will help to keep your birds cool in summer in an indoor aviary, as it can get very hot and stuffy inside. Spraying your birds frequently with water will also keep them cool, and they enjoy that very much: the Bourke might not bathe but loves being sprayed with water. Using a fine spray-gun, as you point the spray upwards towards the roof it will fall down on them like a fine shower. They will soon be back for more!

With an outdoor aviary you should insulate more in the winter months because of the weather. Covering the outer mesh of your aviary panels with plastic and partly boarding them will keep out the wind and rain. Keep regular checks on your aviary, making sure it is sealed off, so that you will not lose any birds.

CAGE BREEDING

Bourkes have been bred in flight cages 1m x 1m x 0.6m (3ft x 3ft x 2ft). This is a suitable size and the most common way to breed the Bourke. A very large cage known as a breeding cage is required so that the bird can exercise by flying perch to perch, the indoor flight protecting them from bad weather. The nest box can be fixed to the outside of the cage with a movable side door so you can look into the nest box to check the progress of the chicks. Make sure that your nest box cannot be knocked down; that could lead to the heartbreak of losing your entire clutch.

I have found cage breeding very successful. By putting one pair in a breeding cage I avoid interference from other Bourkes. Bourkes enjoy their privacy and have produced some lovely chicks when housed in this way.

Bourkes do not seem to need much room to breed; I have bred them in a parrot cage with successful results. I also have an indoor aviary that has been perfect for breeding all my birds, even the cockatiels. It is a good size:

A good sized cage for a pair of Bourkes

1m x 0.6m x 1.3m (3ft x 2ft x 4ft). It has several doors and a space to fit the nest box.

For the floor of my cage I always use woodchip, as I find it much easier to clean, but there are many other materials that you can use; the choice is yours. A tray that slides out for cleaning purposes is fitted to the bottom of the cage. Plenty of small and large wooden perches are placed at different levels. The cage is on wheels for easy moving and cleaning. When cages of this size are used for breeding they become soiled more quickly than aviaries so you will have to clean your cage out daily or every other day.

You may have better results breeding Bourke's parakeets in cages. Birds that are caged can be closely monitored, which

Breeding cage with nest box fitted to the outer side.
Take care that the nest box is firmly attached.

makes it easier to keep records. The best breeding results have been put down to cage breeding. However, it involves more work as, if you are using more than one breeding cage, there is more cleaning and general maintenance work than if you were using an aviary.

CAGE SIZE AND MANAGEMENT

By now you will have noticed that your cage has cost more than the bird itself. Unfortunately, cages can be quite expensive but you can still pick up a secondhand one at a fairly reasonable price. Disinfect it thoroughly before you use it to be sure of killing any germs.

The minimum cage size for a pet parakeet is 50cm x 60cm x 30cm (19in x 24in x 12in). This allows plenty of room for the bird to open its wings full span and is suitable for one Bourke but not recommended for a pair.

Mesh cages are more suitable. Your Bourke would not peck its way out of a wooden cage, as Bourkes do not gnaw, but it would not be so easy to keep clean. However, you must ensure that, if paint has been applied to a mesh cage, it is lead-free; otherwise your bird could be poisoned.

Select the appropriate location for your bird cage. If it is situated in a window area you may have to move the cage around to protect your bird from the glare of the sun and draughts from the window. You can test for draughts with a candle, watching to see if the flame flickers. The kitchen is definitely unsuitable and the most dangerous room in which to keep any bird. Fumes from cooking and household chemicals can seriously damage its health and even lead to death by asphyxiation. The temperature in a kitchen can become uncomfortably hot for any caged bird. Tumble dryers too are dangerous, causing breathing problems for your bird.

Most cages include seed and water containers, but you may need more for different types of food. If you are putting dishes on the floor of the cage, check that they are not in line with the perches so that they will not be fouled by droppings. Dishes that hook onto the mesh of the cage are more suitable. In some cages you can fit seed dishes that slot into a small gap in the cage from the outside. This is a far better idea: not only does it give the bird more room in the cage, but it also keeps the food cleaner, as the bird cannot possibly foul it.

An obviously healthy normal Bourke. The back of a yellow can be seen in the foreground.

Do not overcrowd your cage with too many toys and perches. Make sure your bird has plenty of room so that it can get to its perches and seed dishes safely. Two to three perches are recommended, depending on the size of the cage, and your bird will appreciate it if you provide one thicker one. Perches are made from doweling or unfinished natural wood, and they are about 2cm (3/4in) in diameter. Perches from fruit trees such as apple trees would be the most suitable, but take care to wash them very carefully in case they have been sprayed with insecticide.

Bourkes like to come out of their cages for free flight, and this is important for the bird to ensure that it has enough exercise. However, it can also be very dangerous. Always stick to the following guide lines:

- Shut the door and the windows before you let your bird out of the cage.
- If you keep cats, or any other creatures whose interest in birds might be ambivalent, make sure they are not in the room.
- Close the curtains so that your bird will not bang into the window.
- Try to ensure that the bird is not frightened in any way while it is out. There is always a danger that it will fly into furniture or walls and damage itself and this danger will increase if it panics.
- Only let one Bourke out for exercise at a time, even if they are caged together, as more than one flying free at once can lead to panic.

FEEDING YOUR BOURKE'S PARAKEET

Green foods are a natural source of vitamins and nutrients

FRUIT

Like most tropical birds, Bourke's parakeets like fruit but, like human beings, they do not all have the same likes and dislikes. I have had some that have relished small pieces of grape and apple, whereas others remain uninterested in this, perhaps enjoying grated carrot instead. By offering a variety of fruit you will discover their individual tastes, which will help you with future feeding.

Be careful not to give them too much fresh fruit, as this could cause diarrhoea (see page 44). Should this occur, take them off fruit straight away, starting them on it again when the diarrhoea has cleared up, but in smaller quantities. Keep careful records on the feeding habits of your Bourkes, as these could be very helpful in the future.

Keep to the following rules:

- Wash fresh fruit carefully in case it has been sprayed with chemicals.
- Replace fresh fruits daily, removing any uneaten fruit in case it goes mouldy.

GREEN FOOD

Greens are a natural source of vitamins and nutrients, and essential to your Bourke's diet. As with fruit, taste varies with the individual. Greens should be given in moderation, perhaps starting with a little broccoli, water cress, lettuce or even a (thawed!) frozen vegetable mix. It is quite important that the birds have a selection of greens at least once or twice a week to bring them into prime condition, especially during the breeding months.

Most Bourke's parakeets enjoy grated carrot, but it is not always a favourite, as some positively detest it. As far as wild plants are concerned you can feed them chickweed, which you can usually find in your garden, and dandelions, particularly the darker leaves. These are a natural source of minerals. If for some reason you cannot obtain fresh green food you can buy dried greed food from a pet shop.

Keep to the following rules:

- Wash green foods very carefully. Even if you do not use chemical spays in your own garden, produce might have become contaminated by someone spraying nearby.
- Offer green food in separate dishes.
- Wash dishes carefully before use.
- Do not offer green food that is frosted.

CUTTLEBONE AND MINERAL BLOCKS

Cuttlebone and mineral blocks are an essential element of any bird's diet, vital to its good health. They provide essential protein and vitamins, and the birds thoroughly enjoy them. The mineral block is particularly important during the breeding season, providing calcium to form healthy bones and eggs. A laying hen will demolish a cuttlebone and mineral block in no time.

Cuttlebone and mineral blocks should be available at all times in the aviary or cage. There are various methods of securing them, the main ones being by metal or plastic clips. I prefer plastic clips, or even clothes pegs. Always replace these blocks as soon as they have been consumed. If they have just become soiled they can sometimes be washed rather than replaced.

Keep to the following rules:

- Do not secure cuttlebone beneath perches in case it becomes fouled by droppings.
- Make sure that a supply is always available in the cage or aviary, especially during the breeding months.

GRIT

Since birds do not have teeth, they need some means of breaking up the seed. They do this by eating grit, which is then stored in their gizzards (second stomachs). Here the seed is ground down by means of the grit, and digested slowly. A bird deprived of grit will soon develop digestive problems which could eventually lead to death. Always keep a small dish full of grit in the cage or aviary. The bird only takes it once or twice a week, so it will last for a long time, only needing to be replaced when it is soiled.

If your birds are housed in a cage, you could line the floor with sand mixed with oyster shell, which does the job just as well, but is too expensive to consider for aviary floors. The bird will take all it needs for digesting its food from the cage floor, and the sand will be replaced during normal cleaning.

Keep to the following rules:

- Always have a pot of grit available in the cage or aviary, changing it when it is soiled, or
- Use sand mixed with oyster shell as a cage floor covering, changing it when you clean out the cage

SEED
Seed mixture

Being a grass parakeet, your Bourke will need a mixture of seed, millet, pinenuts and small sunflower seed. You can buy this from your pet shop ready-mixed as Small Parakeet Mix. Some breeders give their birds Canary Mix with added small sunflower and safflower seed.

Grit, mineral blocks and cuttlebone are essential to a bird's diet

Millet spray

This is a great favourite with Bourkes; I have never had one that has not liked it. It should be given to them in moderation as it is very fattening. It is high in protein, which is good when parents are feeding their young. It is also useful when chicks are being weaned as it is easy for the chicks to husk. I give my birds a spray of millet as a treat about twice a week, but they would eat nothing but millet if I let them.

Panicum millet

This is loose millet, off the spray, and is enjoyed just as much as spray millet. It can be mixed with their usual seed or fed separately, and again is useful for weaning chicks.

Sunflower seed

This is also a great favourite with grass parakeets. Since this too is very fattening, especially the white sunflower seed, it should be mixed in small quantities with their normal seed and supplied separately only when you are trying to build them up for breeding.

Hemp

This again is a very popular, fattening seed. Breeders usually provide it during the breeding season, to give their birds the urge to breed and bring them into top breeding condition. Because of its high fat content some breeders withdraw all hemp when the hens have started to lay, but I still mix a small quantity with their normal seed.

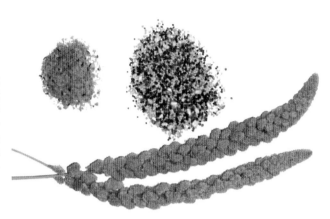

General comments

Keep to these rules:

Your bird will need an assortment of seeds, and you can buy them separately or ready-mixed

- Keep a regular check on your seed, making sure there is a constant supply in the aviary and that the seed is dry and free of dust and droppings.
- Only half-fill the seed containers in your aviary; otherwise the birds cannot reach the seed at the bottom, so there is waste.
- If you can, place seed hoppers rather than pots in your aviary. This again will cut down on waste.
- When you refill your seed container each day, collect the waste together in a container. Every few days you can 'blow' your seed. One method is to use a hair dryer at medium speed on the waste, which will blow away the husk and leave the seed. You will be surprised how much you can save. This is a messy process, best carried out outdoors. A more expensive option is to buy a winnowing machine, but I find that the hair-dryer works perfectly well.

CONDITIONING FOOD FOR BREEDING

Conditioning your birds is essential if you want good breeding results, and this involves providing the correct diet for breeding.

Start conditioning your birds about two months before the breeding season as they need all the conditioning they can get to bring them into top form, and this will include flight. They will need to get used to rearing foods before the breeding season arrives. Special foods include a soft rearing food such as EMP, which can be fed wet or dry. This is appreciated all the year round. Another important one is brown bread, soaked and blended. Cress and sweetcorn are also nutritious and much appreciated. Hard-boiled egg is one of the most important substances, having an extremely high protein content and being full of vitamins required for conditioning. A word of warning: do not leave uneaten egg in the aviary for more than two hours. It goes off incredibly quickly and gives off a terrible smell, particularly in the heat of summer. Breeding Bourke's parakeets also enjoy frozen vegetables, cooked in the microwave and then cooled.

Make sure that you have your rearing food for the chicks at hand right from the beginning, before the breeding actually starts. Altra Mix Shelled is a good mixture; as its name suggests, the seed is shelled, and it is intended for chicks that are being hand-reared, though all the birds like it. It can be blended and added to the food. Some bread and a little milk can also be given to breeding and nesting birds as encouragement to eat, and is also good for the nestlings. Use fresh soft foods every day; never use yesterday's leftovers.

The breeding birds and chicks rely on you for a constant, regular supply of the food they require. Do not let them down; make sure you never run out.

A good seed mix is the basis of your Bourke's diet

All Bourkes love millet but, for the sake of their figures, the supply must be controlled

After the breeding season it is a good idea to build up your birds with some Budgie Tonic to take them up to the next breeding season. This is fattening, but they lose a lot of weight during breeding. However, once breeding starts, you should cut down on fattening items such as Budgie Tonic and hemp, especially the latter. I once put a pot of hemp into the aviary – and found it completely empty after two hours!

As you can see, there are various conditioning foods on which you can feed your parakeets. You can select the ideal one for their needs and tastes by substituting items while keeping the balance right. Conditioning is essential for Bourkes – some birds will not even start nesting if they have not been conditioned.

A breeding pair of normal Bourkes

BREEDING BOURKE'S PARAKEETS

A normal Bourke looking out of its nest box. In the wild, Bourkes nest in holes in trees.

The lifespan of a Bourke's parakeet is 8–12 years, though some have been recorded as living for longer. I have found that it is best not to breed from them until they are a year old, as there is less risk of them abandoning their young at this age. I also feel that it is only fair to retire them for a well-earned rest at about five years, after three to four seasons of breeding.

PAIRING

When you have kept Bourke's parakeets for a while you may decide to breed them. Unfortunately you cannot just put your pair together into the aviary and await results. It just doesn't work like that; I wish it did! And never think you'll become rich by breeding birds. My husband and I do so simply because we enjoy it; the money from the sale of youngsters gets swallowed up in running costs such as the repair of aviaries, food and accessories.

Never breed your birds too young. As I have already said, they should be at least a year old, preferably a little older. Breeding them too young often results in death. The hen frequently becomes egg bound because she is too immature. She is also likely to be prone to disease or nutritional problems because of the needs of her own growing body. Very young birds often desert their chicks because they are just not ready for the responsibilities of parenthood! I have frequently experienced this with a first hatch, although the second might be fine.

If all goes well and you have acquired a cock and a hen that you want to pair, see how they get on with each other before putting a nest box in place. It is best to buy a few pairs and let them pair up as they want. After all, was yours an arranged marriage? Always choose healthy birds with bright eyes and smooth plumage.

Now would be a good time to ring your birds with a coloured split ring, preferably using a different colour for each bird. If your birds are also closed-ringed you will be able to identify them more easily, and record who goes with whom. There is nothing worse than trying to keep your eye on a certain bird when trying to catch it in the aviary – you almost certainly end up catching the wrong one! Coloured rings make them much easier to identify.

Once they have paired off you will see them perching very close together, preening each other, and the cock will be seen to be feeding the hen. Now is the time to take note of the colours or numbers on their rings, record the pairing and possibly transfer the pair from the aviary to a breeding cage.

NEST BOX

At this stage it is worth talking about the nest box, an essential item of equipment. Since the hen will spend several weeks in it, it must be the correct size: 40cm (15in) high, 20cm (8in) wide and 20cm (8in) deep. Bourke's parakeets prefer a tall nest box, and 20cm^2 is the correct base size for a hen rearing a clutch of five eggs; anything less would be over-crowded. It is worth fitting a side door to the nest box, so that you can keep an eye on the chicks. A piece of doweling 5–8cm (3–4in) long should be fitted into the box as a perch just below the entrance hole. Mesh should be attached to the inner wall of the nest box just inside the entrance as a ladder for the chicks when they leave the nest box and to make access easier for the parents. This must be fitted close against the wall and must not turn up at the corners, or the chicks could damage their claws.

NESTING MATERIALS

The most common nesting material is wood shavings with a handful of wood chip on top, about 2.5cm deep. Some breeders prefer to use peat but my Bourkes have always preferred woodshavings. If you decide to use peat, make sure it is Irish moss peat; other peats can be acidic enough to burn the skin of chicks, who are born virtually naked with only a very sparse amount of down.

A nest box of the right size for Bourke's parakeets
(40cm high x 20cm wide x 20cm deep)

COURTSHIP

The courtship between Bourke's parakeets is quite different from that of other birds. They lack two detrimental characteristics present in many parrots: they neither gnaw nor shriek. In addition to this, they are very confiding and can be kept with finches and other smaller species without risk. They communicate constantly with each other, and this is particularly true of the cock.

A rosa Bourke hen incubating her eggs

Like all grass parakeets, Bourkes breed in the spring and summer, although some breeders will breed their birds in small indoor heated aviaries during the winter and then not breed those pairs again during the summer months. By the end of February and the beginning of March, when the mornings are getting lighter, there is less risk of frost, and spring seems to be on the way, you will notice that your pairs are getting ready to breed. Their behaviour will change rapidly, and they will become chirpy, lively and more interested in their mates. You will see them feeding each other and also preening one another, especially around the head and breast areas. They will never seem to be apart, as they thoroughly enjoy each other's company. Like all couples, they have the odd tiff, but they soon return to preen each other as though nothing has happened. The partnership of the Bourke's parakeet is closer than in any other bird I have worked with.

Even out of the breeding season Bourkes remain in their pairs, sitting close to each other, even beak to beak, and you can see them kissing, cooing, snuggling and preening. Bourkes have been known to mate for life and, once paired, they are certainly inseparable.

NESTING

The conditioning foods (see Chapter 2) on which you should have been feeding the birds once they have paired will have brought them into top condition, ready for nesting. I usually start them on these foods for the first month and continue throughout breeding. I certainly condition my birds before putting the nest boxes into the cages or aviaries.

If you see them mate, record the mating in your record book and then supply them with two nesting boxes so that they can choose which one they want as their home. When preparing for mating the hen will lower her back, making it flat so that the cock will find it much easier to mount her by standing on her back. The cock will then begin to swing his tail from side to side under her until their vents meet. The female may squeak softly and the cock bird will murmur very quietly. The whole process can take up to two minutes or more.

Please make sure that you have secured the nest box firmly; it would be heartbreaking for you and the birds to lose a whole clutch by a simple mistake. When you have put the nest boxes in they will probably mate again. If this is the first time you have bred from this pair you can heighten their interest

A pair of rosa Bourkes mating

in the nest boxes by blocking off the entrances with card. This increases their urge to breed and, when you remove the card after a few days, it will not take the cock long to investigate both boxes. They will then investigate them both thoroughly together. Then, around April, they will start calling to each other. The cock will be in and out of the boxes continually for days before he makes his final choice and calls the hen into one of them. When she has entered the box with the cock it generally means that this is the 'desirable residence' chosen. When the choice has been made, take out the other box. I have noticed that a pair of Bourkes does not necessarily pick the same box every year. In my experience, choosing the nest box takes about two weeks, but it could take longer if the birds are not conditioned.

You can expect the first egg 8–10 days from when you first saw them mate. A Bourke's egg is very white and measures roughly 24mm long by 20mm wide. About three days before the hen begins to lay you will notice that she is spending a considerable amount of time in the box. First she will back into a corner, propping her tail on the side of the box and resting her head nearly on the floor. Then she will strain for at least an hour before laying, whereupon she will place the egg in the middle of the nest box floor with her beak. After this, she will lay again, usually every second day, until the clutch of four or five eggs is complete. Serious incubation begins after the first or second egg has been laid, when she tucks the eggs under her breast. Keep careful records so that you are aware of the hatching date. In a mixed aviary you might find that the cock becomes very aggressive at this stage, guarding his nest box against all comers. This is common behaviour during the breeding season.

INCUBATION

The incubation time for Bourke's parakeets is the same as that for most other parakeets: 18–21 days. This varies according to heat and humidity; the greater the ambient temperature, the sooner the hatching. In my experience, incubation is by the hen alone, and she only leaves the nest to empty her bowels and take some calcium and grit, once first thing in the morning and possibly once more during the day. The cock may feed her before she returns to the nest and will keep her supplied with food between times while she is sitting on the eggs.

You will want to monitor the proceedings, but it is important always to let your hen know you are there by whistling or talking softly as you approach the nest box. Tap or scratch gently on the nest box before looking in. Any sudden movement or disturbance could cause her to abandon her eggs or chicks, and then all would be lost.

Do not expect the eggs to hatch in the order in which they were laid. Usually the eggs will hatch every other day, but I have known eggs to hatch on following days or even two eggs on the same day. I have already stressed the importance of keeping records, and it is certainly a good idea to note the laying and hatching dates of the eggs. If there are eggs that are slow to hatch do not remove them too soon; you should allow at least 28 days. The hen will incubate the unhatched egg for at least four weeks before abandoning it completely. Unhatched eggs may contain chicks that have died in the shell for various reasons: the chick could have become chilled or simply been too weak, or the shell could have been too hard or too dry. On average, a chick takes 36–48 hours to hatch. First it makes small fractures around the centre of the egg shell and then it chips away until it is finally hatched.

INFERTILE EGGS

In some clutches you will come across infertile eggs. It is relatively easy to recognise these: a fertile egg is white and an infertile one translucent yellow and not very 'solid'. Leave it alone for 10–14 days, then hold it up to the light, either holding it very gently between your fingers or placing it on a piece of cardboard with a hole slightly smaller than the egg itself cut into it. If the egg is fertile, you should be able to see blood vessels, looking like small veins, appearing in it. These darken as the chicken develops. As you carry out this test, remember that you might have a fertile egg in your hand; it would be heartbreaking to drop it.

If you end up with infertile eggs, they could still be useful. A hen will sometimes temporarily abandon a clutch of fertile eggs and, should this happen, you could give her fertile eggs to a foster mother and place the infertile eggs in her nest box, in case she decides to incubate again. This way, the fertile eggs will still hatch properly, and your hen will have a chance to bring up her chicks.

EGG BINDING

This problem occurs when the hen cannot pass her egg. It is quite a common problem, but very unnerving, as it can lead to the hen's death. It usually happens because of a calcium and vitamin deficiency or breeding in very cold weather, but it can also occur because the hen has been bred too young.

First you will notice your hen on the cage or aviary floor with all the symptoms of a sick bird (see Chapter 2). She will seem completely lethargic and her feathers will be puffed up. She will also be panting continuously. If the egg is not removed within 24 hours she will certainly die. When faced with this situation, you should act as follows:

The hen Bourke usually lays four or five eggs to the clutch, but there are only three in this one

- Wrap the hen in a small towel to restrain her.
- Smear some petroleum jelly (Vaseline) around the vent area, very gently.
- Hold her over some recently-boiled water so that the steam will reach the vent, taking care not to hold her too close. This is called steaming the egg.
- Do not attempt to remove the egg by massage. This could break the egg, which would kill her.
- If steaming does not seem to have any effect on her condition, see your vet straight away.

Should your hen recover, you will have to rest her from further breeding for at least 60 days. If no great damage has been done it should not affect future breeding.

KEEPING RECORDS

I find it is essential to keep records, such as simple notes on who pairs with whom, giving the ring number if they are close-ringed, the colour if they have been split-ringed, or a description of their markings. It can be difficult to describe them by markings, as they can be so alike, and for the same reason it is difficult to know you have caught the right one to check the number on a closed ring. Split, or open, rings come in a wide variety of colours and can be put on the birds at any age, so these are probably the best means of identification for this purpose.

Breeding records can be very important: date of mating, date of first egg, date of when it is due to hatch, size of hatch, illnesses and deaths. All these and many more items can be noted in your records, and may well be useful information for future breeding.

I have found it very useful to number my nest boxes when I am breeding different species in one aviary. This is yet another helpful way of identifying pairing couples and their offspring in your notes.

If your hen becomes egg-bound, it sometimes helps to 'steam' the egg

THE YOUNG BOURKE'S PARAKEET

THE DEVELOPING CHICKS

Congratulations on getting this far! You will be so proud to see the arrival of your chicks and you will be able to follow their progress day by day.

All parakeets are born nearly naked, but with a very sparse covering of soft down (smoke grey for normals, white for rosas). The first 24 hours are critical, and it is essential to check on them regularly during the day (at least three times) to make sure they are all right. The parents will soon get used to you. I lost a chick on one occasion by not checking enough; its crop was full of air, and it subsequently choked and died. This is not uncommon, as the parents tend to feed them enthusi-

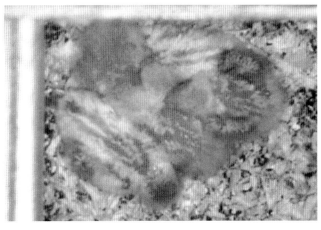

One-week-old rosa chicks

astically and very fast, causing the air to collect in the crop. If you ever find a chick like this, all you can do is to massage the exterior of the crop with your thumb to try to release the air. There is only a 50% chance of saving the chick in such cases.

Once all the chicks have hatched, and the youngest is a few days old and out of danger, the hen will spend more time with the cock out of the nest box. He will still feed her, but not as much, as she will also feed herself now. She exercises constantly to bring herself back into condition again.

Meanwhile, the chicks continue to grow rapidly, doubling their size in a few days. They huddle together to keep warm so, if you see that one has drifted away from the others, put it back with them at once; the cold will soon kill it. Hens have sometimes been known to abandon an individual chick that is weak, leaving it to its death. This is nature's way of preserving the best of the species; the hen will not waste time caring for a chick that will not survive anyway.

In the first week of life the chicks will be fed every hour by their parents. As they progress they will last for two hours, extending to three or four as they get stronger. Obviously, larger amounts can be given to them as they themselves get larger. When they are a few days old you will hear the youngsters chirruping from the nest – a really pleasant sound! As they become older it becomes more frequent and clearer.

When the rosa chicks are six to seven days old they start to develop a grey mask. This becomes more and more pronounced with each day. Their eyes are now open and they are more alert. After seven to eight days you will see the colour start to come through the down (pink in the case of the rosa) and the down will start to disappear.

As the chicks get older, the hen will spend even less time in the nest box with them; she will be more interested in the cuttlebone and mineral block. Her intake will be large, as she will need a great deal to bring her back into condition. The cock will now help feed the chicks, entering the nest box himself to do so, as it is very hard work for the hen. The parents will feed them constantly to fill their crops, so make sure you have a supply of rearing food always available. The hen will gradually become more active, taking more flights to condition herself for nesting once more. She will mate again when the chicks are five or six weeks old, and start to nest as soon as the fully-fledged youngsters have left the nest. She may even start to lay before the youngsters have left the nest, in which case she will get them to 'baby-sit' in her absence by placing the eggs carefully under them for incubation.

When the fledglings have left the nest they are still fed by their parents at first, but gradually less frequently. At six to seven weeks the young are fully weaned, their tail feathers have grown and they can fend for themselves. Now is the time to remove them from the breeding cage or aviary so that the parents can breed again.

If you want your pair to stop breeding for this season, but the hen has laid more eggs while there are still young in the nest, you can interrupt the process by hand-rearing the older chicks and removing the nest box, either fostering or destroying the new eggs. While there is a nest box she will go on laying.

RINGING THE CHICKS

If you are going to put closed rings on your Bourkes, this should be carried out when the birds are six or seven days old, although this will vary with individuals. At this stage, the three long toes will fit through the closed ring. Holding the shorter fourth claw parallel to the leg and the three longer ones straight forward, pass the ring over the front three claws, over the ball of the foot and past the shorter fourth claw until it is released. The ring size for each species is laid down by the British Bird Council, and for the Bourke's parakeet it is Size L.

Never try to force the ring onto the bird after the eighth or ninth day; you will risk serious damage to the chick's claws or leg. As has been mentioned before, this is the best means of identification for a bird. Open or split ringing can be carried out at any age, the ring simply being clipped around the leg.

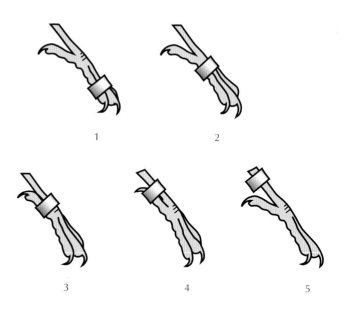

Closed ringing is not the easiest of operations, but it is possible with practice

CLEANING THE NEST BOX

For the first few weeks after the eggs have hatched, the hen will keep the nest box scrupulously clean, removing the droppings with her beak. However, as the birds get older, this standard will be impossible to maintain. The box will become soiled, the droppings sticking to the sides, and they will need to be removed before they harden. From three to four weeks onwards you will have to clean out the nest box or it will start to smell, so you will need a spare nest box or a cardboard box in which to put the chicks while you are doing it. Complete the task as quickly as possible so that you can return the chicks to their parents. In addition to this, your nest boxes should be cleaned and disinfected before use each time. Never use a dirty box, and always spray for mites when setting up.

SEXING YOUR BOURKES

You can sex your Bourkes quite easily when they are about four months old by the shape of their heads. The hen has a flat head that looks like a thumb print, while the cock has a rounded head. The cock's body is slightly bigger than the hen's and, as they come into the breeding season, he will be livelier and more chirpy than usual. The rosa hen has a darker grey mask than the cock, and this can be seen to a lesser extent in the normal and yellow. The top of the normal cock's head will be a lovely shade of blue, and his nostrils and beak will be black, whereas those of the hen will be dull brown.

Another method of sexing your Bourke involves finding out the position of the pelvic bone. This is not very accurate, but some breeders can obtain a true reading this way.

- Hold your bird with its back resting in the palm of your hand so that it is facing upwards.
- Place the little finger of your other hand between the two notches of the pelvic bone.
- If your little finger sits in the small gap, this is a hen ready to breed; if the two notches meet, this is a cock.

This is only accurate on birds at least a year old; the lack of gap can also indicate an immature hen.

WING CLIPPING

If you are intending to tame your bird as a pet, wing clipping will make your task much easier. It only takes about five minutes, and I have had excellent results with it.

You will need:

- a sharp pair of scissors
- a friend to help you
- a pair of gloves (in case the bird nips)

You cannot do this on your own if you are not used to it; someone needs to hold the bird very gently but firmly while the other cuts.

Extend the wing fully. Then, cut all the primary feathers and some of the secondaries. This will ensure that, although the bird will still have limited flight, it will not be able to get very far. The process can then be repeated with the other wing, but this is not absolutely necessary as the bird cannot fly properly when one side has been clipped. This does not affect the appearance of the bird at all.

When cutting the primaries, take great care not to cut too close. If you cut too far under the coverts, especially when the birds are going through a moult, you could sever the tiny blood vessels that are present as new feathers are coming through. Do not be too alarmed if you do so; the bird should not bleed for too long.

If you do not know what you are doing and have no experience, do not attempt wing clipping yourself: ask a veterinary surgeon or experienced birdkeeper to do it for you.

The bird may be rather distressed immediately after its wings have been clipped, especially when it realises it cannot fly properly, but this is only to be expected. It is quite painless and the feathers will grow back with the next moult. Hopefully, your bird will be so used to you by this time that it will not

Wing clipping can help you to tame a young bird but, if you are nervous, ask an experienced birdkeeper for help

struggle to get away. A bird that has not been clipped may become so terrified in the training process that it could fly into glass and break its neck or injure itself in some other way.

I strongly advise you not to clip your bird's wings if there is a cat in the house. If the cat should come into the room while the bird is out (which, of course, shouldn't happen, but accidents do) I'm afraid it would be poultry on the menu for the cat, as the bird couldn't fly out of its way. Your cat's certainly a bird lover, but not in the sense you are!

HAND-REARING

Hand-rearing a Bourke chick is an excellent way of taming it if this is what you want. It is very rewarding but by no means an easy task.

It is best not to take the chick from its parents too young. The parents will do a far better job of rearing very young chicks than you will and are less likely to have fatalities. I would strongly suggest leaving the chick with its parents until its eyes are open or even for two weeks or more, unless there is a good reason not to. I have taken a chick out of the nest box at three to four weeks old and hand-reared it successfully.

A hand-reared Bourke can be a fascinating companion for a child

It is best not to hand-rear from day one but one day you may have to. The parents do sometimes abandon the chicks, and in such a case you would have to do your best. Parents abandon their chicks for a number of reasons. For instance, they may not have been given the correct breeding diet (soft food), they could have been bred too young or they could simply have been disturbed by too much outside interference.

I would not recommend hand-rearing to anyone who does not feel equal to it, as unnecessary hand-rearing has led to many deaths. If you go out to work all day you will not have time to do it; it is a full-time job, requiring your full attention and lots of patience. You should certainly seek professional advice before you start to make sure you are really up to it. Many people have failed in their attempts at hand-rearing, especially when they have started with very young chicks. Chicks are at their most vulnerable during the first 48 hours; each additional hour brings a greater chance of success.

There are many formulas on the market for hand-rearing, two of them being Lakes and Kaytee. You will also need a clean syringe or eye-dropper, both of which you can obtain from your local chemist.

As I have said, a young bird around two weeks old is easiest to work with, especially if you have no previous experience of hand-rearing, as it will not be so afraid of humans. I would suggest an eye-dropper rather than a syringe for very young chicks as a syringe is too big to fit into their beaks. After two weeks it will be better to change to the syringe.

You will find that a chick doubles its size in the first three to four days. Chicks need to be fed at regular times. A chick less than 10 days old will have to be fed every one to two hours. After 10 days it will need to be fed every three hours or so, provided its crop is empty; if it is not, you must wait another hour. The crop is evident as a swelling at the bottom of the bird's neck. If the crop is not empty (in other words, if the chick has not digested its food) to feed it could lead to sour crop infection and the chick could die. Equally, you must not leave the chick with an empty crop for more than three hours. This is the equivalent of us going without food for two weeks, and can again lead to sour crop, this time as a result of starvation.

Mix the formula in a cup with boiled water that has been left to stand for five minutes, following the instructions on the packet very carefully. Mix well, making sure there are no lumps and the formula has dissolved properly, and then pour it into your syringe. If you are feeding more than one chick, make up the required number of syringes and then place them in a cup of pre-boiled water to keep them at the right temperature. You may have to add more hot water to the cup, as the water will cool quickly. Test the formula before feeding just as you would for a baby with a few drops on the wrist. If the formula is too hot it will burn the chick's crop. The chick will let you know if you have it right by its reaction: it will shake its head if the formula is too hot and refuse to open its beak if it is too cold.

Make your chick comfortable while you are feeding it. Do not just put it on the table as this will hurt its legs and it will slide all over the place; put a tea towel or paper towel underneath. You will be able to feed your chick by holding its head between your thumb and forefinger. Be careful not to hurt it by holding too tightly. Then, place the eye-dropper or syringe into the chick's mouth. (You may have to use very gentle force the first time as it will not know what you are trying to do. Once it knows what is coming it will cooperate.) Then, slowly squeeze the contents into the chick's mouth. You will need to massage its crop gently as air collects there. Repeat this about three times for each chick. Their crops will start to fill but only fill them three-quarters full; over-feeding can cause infection and even death. Have a spare syringe with lukewarm pre-boiled water, as you must give each chick a few drops of water by syringe after it has taken the formula – not too much, or you will make it sick.

You may well find that your chicks are wearing half of their dinner. This is very common at this age; as they get older they do not seem to waste any of their food and you can feed them in half the time. Clean your chicks with damp cotton buds, cotton wool or cloths. You must remove all traces of food as this can make them very sore round the beak. Make sure the chicks are not too wet when you put them back. When you have finished feeding, throw all remaining made-up formula away; you must never save it for the next feed. Clean the syringes and rinse them in boiled water ready for the next feed.

There are many options as far as housing your chicks is concerned. You can place them in a cardboard box with a lid and breathing holes. The box should be about 40cm (15in) high so they cannot get out and there should be enough room in the base for them to be comfortable. This is not too much of a problem as they huddle together for warmth and security. A nest box that can be placed inside a large cage is a good idea, just in case they get out of the nest box. Then they will still be safe inside the cage and you won't have birds flying all round the room. A fish tank is another option; breeders sometimes use them for hospital cages. Place a heat pad in the bottom of the cage or tank to keep the chicks warm; younger chicks are more at risk and need plenty of warmth. If your chicks become too hot they will pant constantly with their mouths open and will be scattered around the nest box in an attempt to cool down. By regulating the heat you will make them more comfortable.

In the base of the box you can put a number of absorbent materials. Wood shavings, wood chip and paper towels are all possibilities. Change the material twice a day as it will get soiled quickly. The chicks will deposit their droppings on the side of the box. These are very soft and will stick, so will have to be cleaned off frequently; a dirty box is a breeding-ground for infections. When feeding

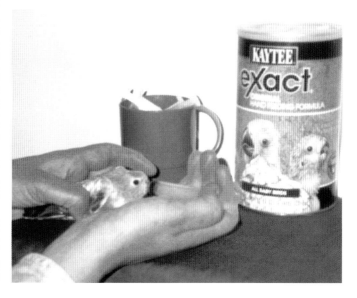

Hand-rearing a three-week-old Bourke

the chicks, only work with one at a time. If you have them all out at once chaos will reign: birds will be flying everywhere and there could be a fatal accident.

The chicks will come to recognise you and think you are their parent, liking the attention when you pick them up. When they are five weeks old you must start to wean them off the formula. This is another stage when you could lose your chicks if you are not careful. After five weeks you should have them in a cage; if their parents were bringing them up they would leave the nest at this stage. Feathers should now be covering the whole body. All the tail feathers should have come through, but will not be quite long enough for full flight until six or seven weeks. The fledglings will exercise by flapping their wings in preparation for their first flight.

Scatter seed and grit on the bottom of the cage so that the chicks can peck at it. You will have plenty of waste when you clean the cage each time but this is to be expected. Start the weaning by cutting out the lunch time feed

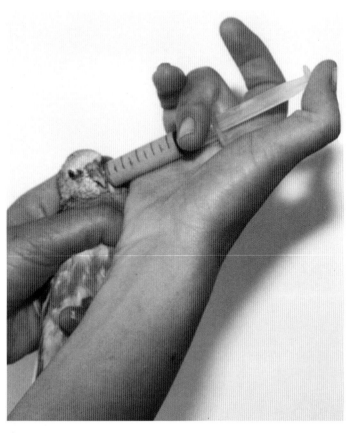

Hand-reared Bourkes become very tame

during the first week. They will begin to try to husk the seed, though they may play around with it at first. This is when I put an adult Bourke with them to encourage them. Hopefully, they will watch the adult bird husk the seed and copy it in feeding and flight. The chicks will watch the adult bird constantly, making your job far easier. After all, you can't get into the cage to show them what you mean!

After another week you will notice they are eating more seed. Then cut out the morning feed, gradually reducing the formula to just an evening feed; they do not want to go to bed on an empty stomach. They should have mastered husking the seed by now, but sunflower is still too hard for them. Put in some spray millet as this is very easy to husk. Panicum millet is also easy and can be supplied in a small dish. You will find this will go down very quickly; it's a great favourite with them. This will encourage them to eat for themselves.

After another week the chicks should be completely off the formula and husking seed for themselves. Do not be too alarmed if they are not all off the formula altogether. There is always one that wants you to go on feeding it. Watch them carefully for at least two weeks to make sure they are feeding themselves properly.

All the constant handling and attention they have received over the weeks will be rewarded when your chicks have turned out just as you wanted them: marvellously tame and affectionate.

My son with his hand-tamed rosa Bourke and cockatiel

35

HEALTHCARE AND ROUTINE MAINTENANCE

Unfortunately, the Bourke's parakeet is not a very hardy bird. Your Bourkes may not become ill very often but, when they do, it must be taken seriously and various procedures must be followed. However, there is a great deal you can do to minimise illness by making sure that they have the right diet, that the cages and aviaries are kept in a clean and hygienic condition and that, should a bird become ill despite all your efforts, it is immediately housed away from the others, preferably in a hospital cage. It is important when you buy new stock to keep it apart from the others for a while until you are sure that it is well.

Most birds require some sort of treatment during their lives. This usually involves providing warmth and high humidity. Warmth can be provided very simply by putting a light bulb close to your cage or a heat pad into the cage. Cover the cage with a towel or tablecloth but leave the front open; natural light is also important. Sometimes warmth alone is enough to put the problem right, but sometimes it can be impossible to cure a sick bird without veterinary assistance. Some illnesses need more medical attention than others.

Spraying for mites is an important part of preventative medicine, and your Bourkes will probably enjoy it

Provided that you care for it properly, your Bourke should live for up to 12 years in captivity

It is not necessary to hold a hand-tame Bourke while you clip its claws,
but do not make any sudden movements

HOSPITAL CAGE

When a bird becomes ill it is best to separate it from your other birds to prevent any diseases or infections from spreading. A purpose-made hospital cage is well worth considering if you have a large quantity of birds. It does not have to be big, as a sick bird will be very lethargic. It is thermostatically controlled, with a temperature range of 29–32°C (85–90°F). Humidity can be increased by putting several pots of water inside the hospital cage and measured with a hydrometer. You will find the Bourke will become more thirsty in the high temperature, and you will need to refill the water pots frequently because of evaporation. All seed and water should be placed near to your bird so that it can reach it without too much effort.

Observe the sick Bourke closely; this is where records can be really useful. A simple health record for each of your birds describing any illnesses and the treatment given can be invaluable when you care for your future stock. If your Bourke does not seem to be recovering, seek help from your veterinary surgeon. Even if it seems to be on the mend, do not be too quick to return it to the aviary; make sure it has recovered completely first. I have used the hospital cage with success in cases of stress, but some illnesses require proper medication prescribed by a vet.

Although I highly recommend hospital cages for sick birds, it must be said that they can be very expensive. Some breeders have made their own small hospital cages, just fitting a light or heat pad inside a cage, and these have proved successful.

PREVENTATIVE MEDICINE
Vitamins and minerals

Vitamins and minerals are essential to our birds' well-being, and they are not always present in sufficient quantities in their normal diet. For this reason we sometimes have to supplement their diets, and the best means is by adding vitamins to their drinking water. Vitamins A and D are found in cod-liver oil and Vitamin E in wheat germ.

A normal Bourke with its distant cousin, the Elegant Grass Parakeet

Chapter 5:

There are certain tell-tale signs that your birds have vitamin or mineral deficiencies, and these include:

- poor appearance of their feathers
- a habit of eating their own droppings
- nails and beaks that do not grow properly
- rather small clutches of eggs
- a variety of breeding problems

Nowadays you can buy various supplements from the pet shop to help keep your birds in top condition and some are already added to seed and formulas. Salt is very important in the breeding season and mineral blocks can be obtained from your pet shop. Vitamins and minerals administered regularly will keep your birds healthy.

Nail clipping

Your Bourke's parakeet may need to have its nails trimmed every so often. This can be a particular problem with cage birds, who are not so active as aviary birds. One way in which you can keep down the rapid growth of their claws is to put emery paper covers on their perches. These are pushed over the perches and are only rough where the claws grip – the birds will sharpen their beaks on them, too! Aviary birds are more at home with natural branches from fruit trees, which will keep their claws a suitable length.

Trimming a bird's nails is a very delicate process. If the bird is nervous and fidgets a lot, there is a risk of taking off too much and making the claw bleed. This can be fatal, as birds do not have much blood. It is very much better to make this a two-person job: one to hold the bird and one to do the clipping.

If (understandably) you are nervous about using scissors, you can buy claw clippers especially designed for birds, and I have often used dogs' nail clippers successfully. Some vets or pet shop assistants will even do it for you for a small fee if you are very nervous.

As you hold the bird's foot over a lamp you will see that there is a small red blood vessel running through the nail but not reaching the end. What you must do is to snip the very end of the nail, avoiding the blood vessel. Claws that have been cut too short will bleed profusely and be very painful for the bird – imagine if you cut your finger nail too short, catching the finger as well! If you have the misfortune to cut too far you can apply non-scented talcum powder, which you can obtain from your chemist. This should stop the bleeding; if it does not, contact your vet.

Hand-reared or hand-tamed birds need not be held. You can clip the claws quite easily as the bird is standing on the perch, and this way it will not become stressed. Take your time and talk to your bird all the time, with no sudden movements (see picture on page 38).

You may find that you have to repeat the process in a few weeks' time, as birds' nails grow quickly, particularly when they have a large intake of calcium.

Worming

Like all grass parakeets, Bourkes are prone to parasitical worms and should be dosed periodically. You should worm your aviary birds twice a year: before the breeding season starts and when it ends. Worms are more common in aviary birds, as the Bourke's parakeet usually picks up food from the bottom of the aviary and, unless the floor is kept scrupulously clean, worms will breed there. If you have many birds in your aviary I would recommend keeping all the dishes off the floor, either on a bench or clipped to the aviary mesh. Seed hoppers are a good thing, as the seed will not become soiled so easily and less will be wasted.

Your cage birds only need to be wormed once a year, starting from when you first purchase them. This is because the cage can be cleaned out more frequently than the aviary.

A variety of products for worming grass parakeets is available from pet shops today. I use Biozine by Harkers, and I administer it by adding it to their water. It is always a good idea to take all the water out

This Bourke may be the picture of health, but steps must be taken to make sure it stays healthy

of the cages about six hours before worming. Then the birds will be thirsty and drink eagerly when you put back the water containing the worming powder, so hopefully each bird will receive the solution. As always, read the instructions on the packet carefully, and then you should not go wrong.

There are indications when your birds have picked up worms. Their wings droop, their eyes are oval in shape and dull and lifeless, their feathers fluff up and they generally look ill; you may even come across a few deaths. If you find birds like this on your aviary floor you must worm them as soon as possible. If you leave them too long they will suffer a considerable weight loss and eventually die. Wormers can be quite expensive but they are very effective.

A yellow forages on a natural branch, watched by a rosa

Spraying for mites

You rarely see scruffy Bourke's parakeets. They do not like bathing, but they thoroughly enjoy taking a 'shower' under a small fine spray gun, 'fired' upwards so that the water falls on them like rain. They open up their wings so that you can spray them all over. It is a good idea to make use of this love of taking a shower by adding a treatment for mites to the water, spraying your birds regularly every season.

So-called 'red' mites are small external parasites that are actually grey until they have sucked blood, and they are a real scourge to birdkeepers. They hide in small cracks in the perches and dark corners of the aviary by day, coming out at night to feed on the blood of their victims, the birds. A bird suffering from this condition spends most of the time scratching itself and may end up by pulling out its feathers because of the irritation. It could suffer from anaemia and also catch an unpleasant disease called lankesterella. All birds can be affected by mites, even young chicks in the nest. The most likely time for infestation is during the hot summer months. Birds kept in the cleanest of environments will become infested with mites so there is no need to be ashamed if your birds become infected; it is almost inevitable. When you spray your birds you should also spray all the perches and all around the aviary. Mites are very prolific and will get anywhere. It is not a good idea to spray the nest boxes while the chicks are still there, but they should be sprayed as soon as the chicks have left the nest. As the spray is only effective against adult mites, not their eggs, you will need to watch carefully and keep on spraying regularly. Remove all seed dishes, water dishes, cuttlebone, mineral blocks and grit from your aviary before you start spraying.

Another form of protection against mites is a 'bird protector'. This consists of a small, hanging plastic container holding insecticide that is harmless to birds but kills mites.

Care during the moult

The juvenile Bourke's parakeet usually moults for the first time at around six months old and you cannot usually sex it until this time. It will moult again a year later, and from then on annually after the spring breeding season. The moult can take several months to complete.

The appearance of your bird's feathers will change according to the weather. In hot weather the feathers are down firmly and appear smooth; in cold weather they are fluffed up to trap the heat in the down and keep the bird warm. Bourke's parakeets can look terrible when they are heavy in moult and the old feathers fall out to make way for the new. Do not worry: this is not an illness or disease. Your Bourke will probably enjoy being sprayed occasionally with tepid water.

Occasionally a bird will suffer from chronic moult. This is usually the result of some dietary deficiency that can be corrected by supplying a more varied diet with a high vitamin content. Plumage spray can also be used to give your bird a better appearance and healthy looking feathers.

INFECTIONS

It is wise to remove a bird showing signs of infection or disease from the aviary or communal cage as soon as you notice it to minimise the risk of spreading illness.

Colds

Colds are commonly mistaken for other illnesses as the symptoms are very much the same as for other infectious diseases.

Bourke's parakeets housed in outdoor aviaries are particularly susceptible to colds and, indeed, any other infections during winter. Just like humans, Bourkes usually start their colds with sneezing and nasal discharge (runny nose) or blocked nostrils. Other symptoms are eyes half open, ruffled feathers and poor appetite. A bird that never preens itself is also very likely to have something wrong with it. Do not ignore these symptoms as colds can turn into pneumonia with severe respiratory difficulties. The symptoms can be made worse by sudden temperature drops and draughts. Your bird will also become lethargic and will probably be on the bottom of the cage, and it could also go into stress, followed by shock, and die. The bird will become tame during the illness and you will be able to handle it with no problem.

Your first step must be to transfer such a bird from the aviary to a hospital cage, purpose-made or improvised, as described earlier in this chapter. Warmth is the only real cure for this condition. The bird could need to stay there for a few days. If you are using an ordinary cage heated by a lamp, do not turn off the lamp at night, as this could be fatal. Make sure the patient has recovered fully before you return it to the aviary and keep a close eye on it for a few more days. Be ready to return the bird to the hospital cage at the first sign of a relapse. If the treatment does not produce any improvement, consult your vet; your bird may need prescribed antibiotics for a full recovery. These will usually be administered by adding them to its water or seed.

I have found that birds can catch the common cold from humans and, as I have already said, the symptoms are remarkably similar.

Aspergillosis

This is a mould infection which can be minimised by basic hygiene. It is vital to give your birds clean seed, making sure it is not mouldy. When spilt seed hulls, fruit and greens mingle with droppings on the aviary floor, along with spilt water and condensation, a mould will almost certainly form. This must be removed; aspergillosis carries a high chance of respiratory infection and there is no complete cure.

Eye infections

As I mentioned before, dirty perches spread infection. Bourke's parakeets are especially prone to eye infections as they have a habit of rubbing their heads side-to-side on the perches to scratch their beaks: not a good idea if the perches are dirty! As in the case of all other infections, it is best to isolate the sufferer, as the infection can pass quickly from bird to bird.

One breeder tells me that he has successfully cured this condition by holding a wet tea-bag over the eye but I have yet to try this. Bathing the eye sometimes helps. Apply warm water with a very small pinch of salt added, using a ball of cotton wool and dabbing very gently. Fresh cotton wool must be used for each eye every time so that you do not spread the infection. If there is no improvement consult your vet; prescription-only medicines may be required.

Diarrhoea

During your time as a birdkeeper you are bound to come across this condition at some time. It can be caused by the slightest thing. The first symptom will be abnormal droppings, which will usually be green and watery and could have small spots of blood in them. The bird can be also seen hunched up on the bottom of the cage or aviary.

Pet Bourke's parakeets that are kept indoors are up against various dangers. Many house plants can cause this condition as can substances such as alcohol, butter, cheese, rotten foods or unclean water which the bird might encounter as it flies around. The aviary bird can suffer by being housed in unhygienic conditions; how often you clean the aviary and food dishes is a major factor. However, incorrect diet is the most common cause of diarrhoea. In particular, diarrhoea can be caused by too much fruit and greens, so these should be removed from the cage or aviary at once if you notice watery droppings. This can then be treated as mild diarrhoea, which should not cause too much alarm as it is unlikely to develop into a fatal condition.

Diarrhoea needs to be monitored carefully as it can be a symptom of various illnesses. Keep regular checks on the birds' faeces. If ever you notice any traces of blood in the faeces, this may be more serious, so I would recommend consulting your vet. In milder cases, you can treat the bird yourself with Johnson's Avol Mixture, a treatment for loose stools. Just add half a teaspoonful to the water for three or four days, changing it daily. The vent area will become very soiled and unpleasant and you must keep it clean by frequent washing with warm water.

In severe cases, the hospital cage will be required and you will need to visit your vet for antibiotics.

A healthy breeding pair of rosas

further reading

Budgerigars: your easy guide to training
Paula Jones and Philippa Bower

If you are interested in training your young budgerigar to sit on your hand, fly freely around the room and to speak, then this is the book for you. Drawing on their experience with the talented Rainbow, the authors have written a delightful book to help with all the above. Humourously illustrated, the book will appeal to everyone who has tried or wants to try to give their budgie the best life possible.

ISBN 1 85279026-1

Diseases of Cage Birds
Elisha W Burr, DVM, *editor*

Dr Burr is one of the world's outstanding authorities on cage bird diseases. For this book, aimed at the serious aviculturist, he has gathered a group of experts to write about all aspects of cage bird health, diseases, management and breeding. The result is an accumulation of expert knowledge on bird disease covering a wide range of species and situations. The book is illustrated with colour photographs and diagrams to help the reader to identify problems if they occur.

ISBN 0 86622 945 0

Bird Keeping: for the young and young-at-heart
John Earley

Why have birds been kept as pets for about 5000 years? Because they are easy to care for and make inexpensive, active and colourful companions. This book helps you to choose the best bird for you, tells you how to look after it, and gives you lots of interesting facts about your hobby. John Earley, an established writer about cage and aviary birds, is perhaps best known as the creator of 'Chirpy', an instructional character featured in the magazine *Bird keeper*. Chirpy is your guide in this book too, and Gordon Parkinson, the artist, succeeds in making Chirpy as amusing as he (or she) is informative.

ISBN 1 85279027X

All the above books, and more, are available from
TFH/Kingdom Books, PO Box 15, Waterlooville P07 6BQ, England

If you have any general enquiries about keeping birds, helpful advice
can be obtained from the following address:
National Council for Aviculture
4 Haven Crescent
Werrington
Stoke-on-Trent
Staffs   ST9 0EY

index